WILDFLOWERS

AUSTRALIA

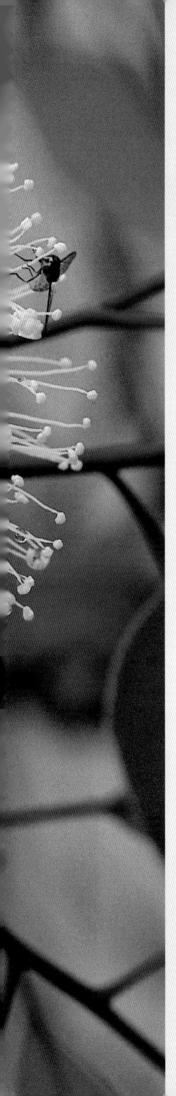

C o n t e n t s

Cover and opposite: *Pear-fruited Mallee* (Eucalyptus pyriformis).
Inside front cover: *Finke River Mallee* (Eucalyptus sessilis).

Introduction

When Australia separated from the Gondwana landmass about 45 million years ago, it carried within its warm, humid forests the ancestors of modern-day plants and animals. These life-forms evolved in the ever-changing environment as Australia continued its northward drift. By 20 million years ago conditions were much the same as they are today and flowering plants had developed unique ways of coping with the continent's cooler and drier environments.

Over half of the 18 500 flowering plant species identified in Australia so far are found nowhere else. The distinctive Australian look of many of these wildflowers is the outward evidence of their genetic and evolutionary inheritance.

Flowers are a plant's means of achieving fertilisation to produce seeds for a new generation. Transferring genetic material between plants of the same kind increases a plant's adaptability to environmental change. Being rooted to the ground, plants largely depend on animals to carry that genetic material via pollen. Plants offer inducements to perform this task: food, nesting materials and a place to rest or lay eggs.

Flowers boldly advertise their attractions through colours, scents, shapes and patterns that appeal to animal senses. The features that make flowers such successful advertisers also contribute to their appeal to humans.

Opposite: *Red and Green Kangaroo Paw* (Anigozanthos manglesii).
Above: *Geraldton Wax* (Chamelaucium uncinatum).

Places to live

Armed with strategies developed in isolation over millions of years, flowering plants have spread throughout Australia, from mountain top to river valley, from seashore to inland plain. Australia's climate, landforms and geology create a host of environments that provide the sunlight, water, soil and space necessary to plant life.

As a place to live, however, the continent's habitats seem rather harsh. Its ancient soils are poor in nutrients. Humid environments are limited, 70 per cent of the country being arid or semi-arid. The dry temperate habitats that dominate Australia are also fire-prone. Yet some 18 500 species of flowering plants manage to thrive on what the country has to offer.

Adaptability and diversification have been key factors in the remarkable success of flowering plants in Australia. Millions of years of dynamic evolutionary processes have equipped plants such as wattles and eucalypts with various mechanisms to reduce water loss, recover from fire and even fix nitrogen in the soil. With the added benefits of diversity, some groups, such as grevilleas, have representatives in most habitats, wet or dry, tropical or temperate.

Opposite: *Flowering shrubs anchor the sandhills near Uluṟu.*
Above: *Wildflowers carpet mulga shrubland in central Australia.*

Top: *Rain brings a flush of ephemeral wildflowers to the sandplains below Mt Augustus, WA.*

Above: *Massed plantings of wildflowers at Kings Park soften the Perth cityscape.*

Top: *Coastal heath at Nambung National Park, WA.*

Above: *The sandhills of the Pilbara, WA, burst into colour after monsoon rains.*

Opposite: *Bottlebrushes flourish beneath an east-coast forest of eucalypt trees.*

Above, top to bottom: *Banksia shrubland in south-western Australia; spring-flowering wattles in an open forest; a colourful woodland understorey.*

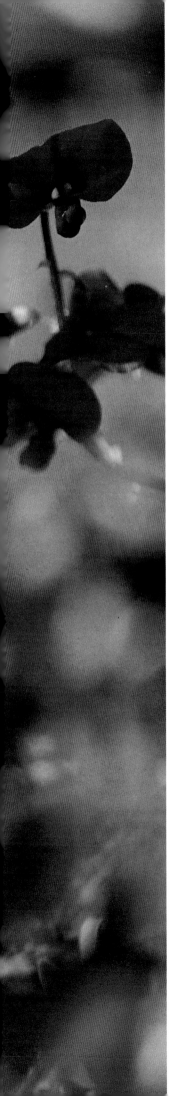

A world of colour

Eye-catching colours contribute much to the beauty of Australian wildflowers. The saturated red of a Sturt's Desert Pea, the intense yellow of massed wattle blossoms, the stunning blue of a Scented Sun Orchid leap out from sun-bleached backgrounds and grab attention.

Different arrangements of tiny pigment cells in plant sap reflect and absorb light, producing colours of varying intensity. Some flowers have no pigment cells and air between the colourless petals creates an illusion of white. Wildflower colours match the visual abilities of animal pollinators. The greater a flower's visual impact, the easier and quicker it is for an animal to home in and reap its reward.

The rainbow of colours that so delights human eyes goes largely unseen by the insects that pollinate nearly 80 per cent of flowering plants. Where humans see red, most insects only see black – they have ultraviolet vision. Yellow, blue and ultraviolet are basic insect "colours" that combine to form many flower colours, some invisible to humans.

Some birds, mammals and butterflies have red-sensitive vision, and Australia's many red-hued flowers appeal to these important pollinators.

Flower colour has benefits aside from pollination. Sunscreening purple pigments protect delicate tissues from those same ultraviolet rays that make flowers attractive to insects.

Opposite: *Sturt's Desert Pea* (Swainsona formosa).
Above: *Round-leaved Parakeelya* (Calandrinia remota).

Top: *Yellow Flag* (Patersonia umbrosa *var.* xanthina).

Above: *A mosaic of Dampiera, Helichrysum and Helipterum species.*

Top: *Banks of wildflowers enliven spring in Kings Park, Perth, Western Australia.*

Above: *Starflowers* (Calytrix leschenaultii).

Clockwise from top: *Western Bloodwood* (Eucalyptus terminalis); *Scented Sun Orchid* (Thelymitra aristata);
Graceful Cassia (Senna venusta).

Clockwise from top left: *Many-flowered Fringe Lily* (Thysanotus multiflorus); *Wavy-leaved Hakea* (Hakea undulata); *Tasmanian Heath* (Epacris *sp.*).

Clockwise from top left: *Long Purple Flag* (Patersonia occidentalis); *Common Spider Orchid* (Caladenia patersonii); *Hairpin Banksia* (Banksia spinulosa); *Sand Bottlebrush* (Beaufortia squarrosa).

Clockwise from top left: *Prickly Dryandra* (Dryandra falcata); *Morning Iris* (Orthrosanthus laxus); *Little Bottlebrush* (Beaufortia micrantha); *colour variation of Everlasting Daisy* (Bracteantha bracteata).

A touch of texture

The element of texture adds much to the visual beauty of wildflowers. Humans are very sensitive to touch, and the textures of flowers evoke tactile comparisons with familiar objects – papery everlasting daisies, bristly bottle-brushes, furry kangaroo paws.

Texture or lustre comes from the structure of the individual parts of a flower. If the petal surface is smooth, a flower looks shiny or metallic. The mirror effect of a starch layer within a petal makes a flower shine too. Hairy or warty petal surfaces produce a matt or velvet effect. A waxy surface film dulls a petal's lustre and tones down its colours. Grevilleas, callistemons and hakeas have tiny petals and their typical bristly look comes from the female stamens, which stand above the other flower parts.

From an animal's viewpoint, texture enhances the attractiveness of a flower's colour and shape. It also offers tactile stimulation when petal grooves guide tongues seeking nectar. Drakaea orchids, for example, look, smell and feel like female Thynnid wasps. The male mistakenly tries to mate with the flowers, thereby cross-pollinating them.

Texture plays other strategic roles in plant survival. Hairy petals insulate delicate tissues; waxy ones reduce water loss. And the dead sounding rustle of papery daisies just might save them from browsing plant eaters.

Opposite: *Pink Everlasting Daisy* (Rhodanthe chlorocephala *var.* rosea), *also called "Rosy Sunray".*
Above: *Marri* (Eucalyptus calophylla).

Clockwise from top: *Red-flowering Gum* (Corymbia ficifolia); *Wallum Fringe* (Nymphoides exiliflora); *Poached Egg Daisy* (Polycalymma stuartii).

Clockwise from top: *Desert Peaflower* (Swainsona maccullochiana); *golden spikes of wattle;*
White Foxtail (Ptilotus latifolius).

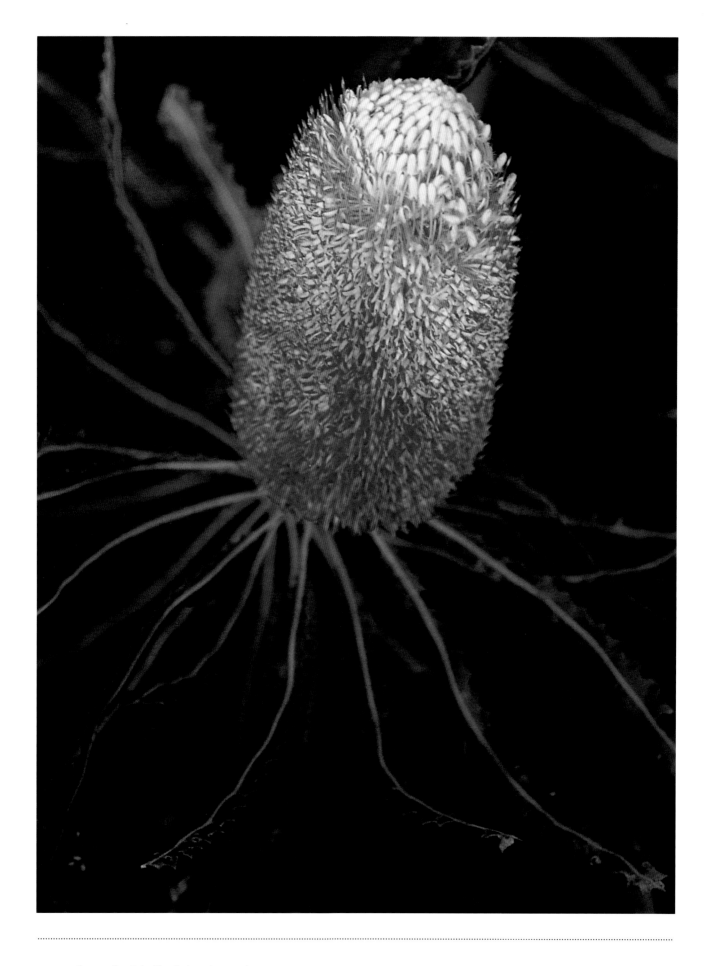

Orange Banksia (Banksia prionotes).

Clockwise from top: *Mottlecah* (Eucalyptus macrocarpa); *Annual Yellowtop* (Senecio gregorii); *Purple Enamel Orchid* (Elythranthera brunonis).

Shape by design

For centuries flowers have been an inspiration to artists, artisans and architects who have used stylised flower shapes as symbolic and decorative motifs. Australians are no exception, and our wildflowers appear on everything from the national coat of arms to bed-linen.

A flower's shape can help the plant to protect its reproductive organs. The shape can also facilitate fertilisation by matching an animal's vision and food-gathering abilities.

The number, size, structure and arrangement of a flower's parts decide its shape. Individual flower shapes range from simple open circles, bells and tubes to the complex, bizarre shapes of orchids that resemble insects, mushrooms and even dung.

New dimensions are added to form when basic flower shapes appear in massed arrangements called inflorescences. Again, the variety is immense but overall the shapes are open or elongated. An everlasting daisy has a centre of small, tightly packed flowers that are surrounded by rows of petal-like leaves. Thousands of crowded flowers that open sequentially from bottom to top create a cone-shaped banksia spike. On a cylindrical bottlebrush spike, the flowers open at the same time. Inflorescence is common in Australian wildflowers and is especially suited to flying insects and the brush-tipped tongues of honeyeaters, lorikeets, fruit bats and honey possums.

Opposite: *Fuchsia Heath* (Epacris longiflora).
Above: *Golden Penda* (Xanthostemon chrysanthus).

Fringed Mantis Orchid (Caladenia dilatata *var.* falcata).

Cranbrook Bell (Darwinia meeboldii).

Clockwise from top: *Eremophila* (Eremophila maculata *var.* brevifolia); *Wavy Marshwort* (Nymphoides crenata); *Tinsel Flower* (Cyanostegia corifolia).

Clockwise from top left: *Showy Banksia* (Banksia speciosa); *Heath Banksia* (Banksia ericifolia); *Native Rhododendron* (Rhododendron lochae).

Clockwise from top left: *Yellow Flag* (Patersonia umbrosa *var.* xanthina); *Victorian Heath* (Epacris impressa); *Swamp Banksia* (Banksia littoralis); *Swamp Orchid* (Phaius tankervilleae).

Clockwise from top left: *Sunbursts of wattle flowers; Cooktown Orchid* (Dendrobium bigibbum); *Giant Water Lily* (Nymphaea gigantea); *Crimson Kunzea* (Kunzea baxteri).

Pattern with purpose

Endless patterns can be found in the repetitions, sequences and contrasts of wildflower shapes and colours. But pattern, like beauty, is in the eye of the beholder. For insects with ultraviolet vision, special guide-marks appear on nearly half of all flowers. The human eye, however, sees those contrasting lines, dots and patches on only about a quarter of all flowers.

Combinations of guide-marks, colours and shapes create patterns that the insect brain registers and stores. Pattern helps an insect see its target flower from a distance and home in on its centre, where the insect claims a food reward in exchange for dropping off and picking up pollen.

Converging lines along flower petals are a common guide-mark. These are usually a dark or contrasting colour, but they can be structural grooves. Contrasting petal tips and a dark central patch on an open-shaped flower produce a pattern of concentric circles. To an insect, the spots on the inner surface of a tubular flower resemble stamens and are an invitation to investigate. When guide-marks change colour after fertilisation, an insect stops visiting because its stored image does not fit the flower's new pattern.

The downside to pattern in terms of plant survival occurs when a flower pattern is so specialised that it attracts only one kind of insect. The plant's chances of producing a new generation are diminished if the right pollinator fails to appear during flowering time.

Opposite: *Scarlet Banksia* (Banksia coccinea).
Above: *Detail of a grevillea flower spike.*

Peaflower (Hovea *sp.*).

Green Birdflower (Crotalaria cunninghamii).

Clockwise from top left: *Pincushion Cone Flower* (Isopogon dubius); *Swamp Daisy* (Actinodium cunninghamii); *Geraldton Wax* (Chamelaucium uncinatum); *Southern Cross* (Xanthosia rotundifolia).

Top: *White Banjine* (Pimelea ciliata).

Above: *Gungurru* (Eucalyptus caesia).

Clockwise from top left: *Cowslip Orchid* (Caladenia flava); *Albany Bottlebrush* (Callistemon glaucus); Hakea *sp.;* *Honey myrtle* (Melaleuca *sp.*).

Top: Pentachondra pamila.

Above: *Waratah* (Telopea speciosissima).

Behind the photographs

Nothing gives me more joy than to wander alone, camera in hand, over a desert dune or through heathland bush. I like to be as unencumbered as possible so that I can drop to my knee or lie on the sand to marvel at the beauty of one of Australia's spectacular wildflowers.

Use of a motor drive lets me keep one hand free, maybe to hold grasses back from my focus point, or, especially in low light, use it to brace the camera for a slow shutter speed. I sometimes use a tripod for stability, but prefer not to as the contraption slows movement and hinders my ability to change my viewing perspective easily.

I rarely, if ever, use flash for either total or fill-in light, preferring to use natural light for softer colours. My wildflower photographic work brings out my feminine side: I see flowers as very erotic and often stimulating to all the senses, especially the sense of smell.

I use 200 mm and 105 mm macro lenses most of the time, even a 500 mm lens. I favour the 200 mm lens: its longer focal length enables me to create a soft, out-of-focus background. This softer background to an image helps isolate the flower, which may be quite cryptic and similar in colour to the background itself.

My camera of choice is the Nikon F5, with Kodak's VS 100 a.s.a. film, but recently I also began to film wildflowers with a digital video camera.

Opposite: *Setting up with a tripod (top) and a hand-held rig (bottom).*
Above: *Perfection of contrast – White Foxtail bush against red sand.*

Clockwise from top left: *A grasshopper investigates a Lotus Lily* (Nelumbo nucifera); *Brown Honeyeater on Red Kangaroo Paw* (Anigozanthos rufus); *New Holland Honeyeater probes a bottlebrush; Sugar Glider and bottlebrush; Pygmy-possums and Coastal Banksia.*

In daylight

and in darkness

noisy, gaily coloured

and silent, big-eyed creatures

move from tree to tree

creating

in their path

a mystery.

STEVE PARISH

Top: *A Sugar Glider feeds on a Coastal Banksia.*

Above: *Rainbow Lorikeet and Golden Penda* (Xanthostemon chrysanthus).